Cursive Handwriting Workbook for Adults

Advanced Cursive Writing Worksheets with Intriguing Science Facts for a Meaningful Practice

Introduction to Advanced Cursive Handwriting

The goal of this workbook is to help you improve your handwriting skills to an expert level. It contains exercises for rewriting entire paragraphs and sentences (multiple times if possible). The font size is smaller compared to other standard children's practice worksheets.

This book also contains a short practice section for each letter. I recommend you complete this section first and practice each individual letter, before moving to the actual exercises. This section also includes recommendations on how each letter should be written. The rest of the workbook contains intriguing science facts from various fields like:

- *astrology*
- *anatomy*
- *engineering*
- *physics*
- *recycling*
- *zoology*
- *and many, many more...*

At the beginning of each worksheet, you will find the sentence written in a traceable cursive font, after that you should use the remaining space to rewrite the entire sentence again (at least once).

In order to obtain the most value out of this workbook, you should not only practice your cursive handwriting but also improve your knowledge by learning from the short facts presented in this book. Each sentence is concise and easy to remember. Learning interesting facts from various scientific fields can help you start meaningful conversations with friends and family in your day to day life.

Cursive uppercase letters

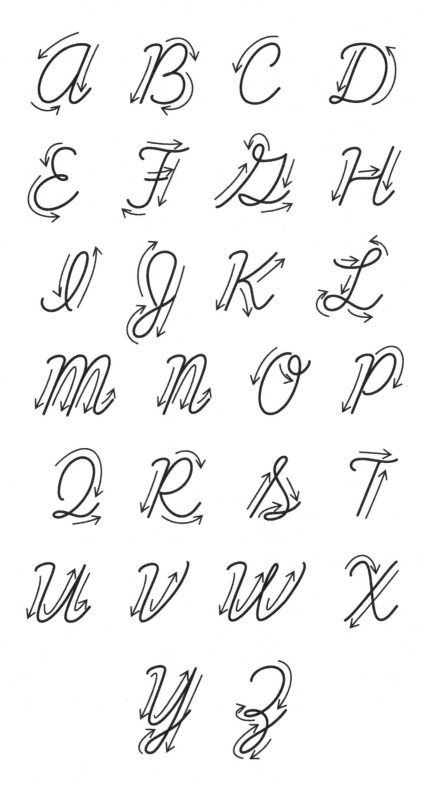

Cursive lowercase letters

Cursive letter practice

a

a

B

b

C

c

D

d

E

e

F

f

G

g

H

h

I

i

J

j

K

k

L

l

M

m

N

n

O

o

P

p

Q

q

R

r

S

s

T

t

U

u

V

u

W

u

X

x

Y

y

Z

z

Science Fact #1:

The hot liquid rock located under the surface of the Earth is called magma. It is only called lava once it comes out onto the surface.

The hot liquid rock located under the

surface of the Earth is called magma.

It is only called lava once it comes

out onto the surface.

Science Fact #2:
Natural gas doesn't have an odor. Humans add strong smells to
it so they are able to detect leaks when they occur.

Natural gas doesn't have an odor.

Humans add strong smells to it so

they are able to detect leaks when

they occur.

Science Fact #3:

Hawaii and Japan are located on two different tectonic plates. They are moving towards each other at a speed of 10 cm per year.

Hawaii and Japan are located on two different tectonic plates. They are moving towards each other at a speed of 10 cm per year.

Science Fact #4 :

The world's largest desert is called the Sahara and it covers about one third of Africa.

The world's largest desert is called the

Sahara and it covers about one third

of Africa.

Science Fact #5:
The Nile River is the longest river on Earth. It has a length of
6650 kilometres (4132 miles).

The Nile River is the longest river

on Earth. It has a length of 6650

kilometres (4132 miles).

Science Fact #6:

The only rock that can float in water is a volcanic rock known as pumice.

The only rock that can float in water

is a volcanic rock known as pumice.

Science Fact #7:

The highest mountain on Earth is Mount Everest. Its peak reaches 8848 meters (29029 feet) above sea level.

The highest mountain on Earth is

Mount Everest. Its peak reaches

8848 meters (29029 feet) above sea

level.

Science Fact #8:
The saltiest ocean located on Earth is the Atlantic Ocean.

The saltiest ocean located on Earth is the Atlantic Ocean.

Science Fact #9:

Scientists date the Earth as being between 4 and 5 billion years old.

Scientists date the Earth as being between 4 and 5 billion years old.

Science Fact #10:

The largest tropical rainforest on Earth is called the Amazon rainforest.

The largest tropical rainforest on Earth is called the Amazon rainforest.

Science Fact #11:

The largest living structure in the world is the Great Barrier Reef, which is located in the Coral Sea in Australia.

The largest living structure in the world is the Great Barrier Reef, which is located in the Coral Sea in Australia.

Science Fact #12:

The bottom of the Grand Canyon contains rock that is around 2 billion years old.

The bottom of the Grand Canyon
contains rock that is around 2
billion years old.

Science Fact #13:

The hottest planet in our solar system is Venus. Its surface temperature reaches over 450 degrees Celsius.

The hottest planet in our solar system is Venus. Its surface temperature reaches over 450 degrees Celsius.

Science Fact #14 :
Our solar system is around 4.6 billion years old.

Our solar system is around 4.6 billion

years old.

Science Fact #15:

Uranus is the only planet in our solar system that rotates on its side like a barrel.

Uranus is the only planet in our solar system that rotates on its side like a barrel.

Science Fact #16:

Venus is the only planet that spins in the opposite direction to the other planets.

Venus is the only planet that spins in the opposite direction to the other planets.

Science Fact #17:

The Russian satellite, Sputnik, was the first man-made object to be sent into space. The event occurred in the year 1957.

The Russian satellite, Sputnik, was
the first man-made object to be sent
into space. The event occurred in the
year 1957.

Science Fact #18:
Europa, Ganymede, Callisto and Io are the 4 largest moons of
Jupiter.

Europa, Ganymede, Callisto and Io
are the 4 largest moons of Jupiter.

Science Fact #19:

Oceans cover around 70% of the Earth's surface.

Oceans cover around 70% of the

Earth's surface.

Science Fact #20:
The Pacific Ocean is surrounded by a large number of active volcanoes known as the Pacific Ring of Fire.

The Pacific Ocean is surrounded by a large number of active volcanoes known as the Pacific Ring of Fire.

Science Fact #21:

In 1932, Amelia Earhart became the first female to fly solo across the Atlantic Ocean.

In 1932, Amelia Earhart became
the first female to fly solo across
the Atlantic Ocean.

Science Fact #22:
The Arctic Ocean is almost completely covered in sea ice during
the winter.

The Arctic Ocean is almost completely
covered in sea ice during the winter.

Science Fact #23:

The speed of light in a vacuum is around 300,000 kilometres per second (186,000 miles per second).

The speed of light in a vacuum is around 300,000 kilometres per second (186,000 miles per second).

Science Fact #24:
Light travels from Earth to the Moon in 1.255 seconds.

Light travels from Earth to the
Moon in 1.255 seconds.

Science Fact #25:

The process used by plants to convert carbon dioxide into food is called photosynthesis, and it uses energy from sunlight to do this.

The process used by plants to convert carbon dioxide into food is called photosynthesis, and it uses energy from sunlight to do this.

Science Fact #26:
Bamboo can grow almost 1 meter (3.28 feet) in a single day.

Bamboo can grow almost 1 meter
(3.28 feet) in a single day.

Science Fact #27:
Currently, humans have identified over 200,000 plant species
and the list is still growing.

Currently, humans have identified

over 200,000 plant species and the

list is still growing.

Science Fact #28:

The Mariana Trench is the deepest known point in the world's oceans. It is found in the Pacific Ocean.

The Mariana Trench is the deepest

known point in the world's oceans.

It is found in the Pacific Ocean.

Science Fact #29:
In space, humans become a little taller because there's no gravity pulling them down.

In space, humans become a little

taller because there's no gravity

pulling them down.

Science Fact #30:

During a lightning strike, surrounding air is heated rapidly which causes it to expand faster than the speed of sound. This causes thunder.

During a lightning strike, surrounding air is heated rapidly which causes it to expand faster than the speed of sound. This causes thunder.

Science Fact #31 :
Sound cannot travel through a vacuum.

Sound cannot travel through a

vacuum.

Science Fact #32 :
The speed of sound is approximately 1230 kilometres per hour (767 miles per hour).

The speed of sound is approximately 1230 kilometres per hour (767 miles per hour).

Science Fact #33:

Sound travels four times faster through water than it does through air.

Sound travels four times faster

through water than it does through

air.

Science Fact #34:

A 200-pound man would only weigh 76 pounds on Mars. This is caused by the differing gravitational pulls of the two planets.

A 200-pound man would only

weigh 76 pounds on Mars. This is

caused by the differing gravitational

pulls of the two planets.

Science Fact #35:
When traveling at a speed of 80 kilometres per hour (50 miles per hour), a car uses around half of its fuel just to overcome the wind resistance.

When traveling at a speed of 80 kilometres per hour (50 miles per hour), a car uses around half of its fuel just to overcome the wind resistance.

Science Fact #36:
It's believed that the Earth's core is a mix of iron and nickel.
This causes the Earth to have its own magnetic field.

It's believed that the Earth's core is

a mix of iron and nickel. This causes

the Earth to have its own magnetic

field.

Science Fact #37:
An electromagnet is created by an electric current running through a surrounding coil.

An electromagnet is created by an
electric current running through a
surrounding coil.

Science Fact #38:
The solar wind is deflected by the Earth's magnetic field.

The solar wind is deflected by the
Earth's magnetic field.

Science Fact #39:

Despite its size, a hippopotamus can run faster than a man.

Despite its size, a hippopotamus can run faster than a man.

Science Fact #40:
Electric eels can cause electric shocks of around 500 volts.

Electric eels can cause electric shocks
of around 500 volts.

Science Fact #41:

The Cheetah is the fastest land animal on Earth. Its maximum speed is around 113 km per hour (70 miles per hour).

The Cheetah is the fastest land animal on Earth. Its maximum speed is around 113 km per hour (70 miles per hour).

Science Fact #42:
The Killer Whale, also known as the Orca, is actually
a type of dolphin.

The Killer Whale, also known as the
Orca, is actually a type of dolphin.

Science Fact #43:
Giant Water Lilies can grow over 1. 8 meters (6 feet) in
diameter.

Giant Water Lilies can grow over

1. 8 meters (6 feet) in diameter.

Science Fact #44:
Cows and horses sleep while standing up.

Cows and horses sleep while standing

up.

Science Fact #45:

Female lions are better hunters than male lions.

Female lions are better hunters than

male lions.

Science Fact #46:

The Elephant is the largest land-based mammal on Earth.

The Elephant is the largest land-based mammal on Earth.

Science Fact #47:
A shape with 20 sides is called an icosagon.

A shape with 20 sides is called an

icosagon.

Science Fact #48:

Before the 16th century, math equations were written in words which made it a very time-consuming process. After that, mathematical symbols were invented.

Before the 16th century, math
equations were written in words which
made it a very time-consuming
process. After that, mathematical
symbols were invented.

Science Fact #49:
An Olympic gold medal is made mostly of silver.

An Olympic gold medal is made
mostly of silver.

Science Fact #50:

The dimples found on a golf ball allow it to fly further than it would without dimples. This is because the dimples help to reduce drag.

The dimples found on a golf ball

allow it to fly further than it would

without dimples. This is because the

dimples help to reduce drag.

Science Fact #51:
The official distance of a marathon is 42.195 kilometres
(26.219 miles).

The official distance of a marathon
is 42.195 kilometres (26.219 miles).

Science Fact #52:

The fastest recorded tennis serve exceeded 250 kph (155 mph).

The fastest recorded tennis serve

exceeded 250 kph (155 mph).

Science Fact #53:

Snowboarders and ice skaters glide on a thin layer of water while traveling. This is because their skates and boards heat the snow beneath them.

Snowboarders and ice skaters glide on a thin layer of water while traveling. This is because their skates and boards heat the snow beneath them.

Science Fact #54:

Scientists believe that the moon was used as a form of calendar as far back as 6000 years ago.

Scientists believe that the moon was used as a form of calendar as far back as 6000 years ago.

Science Fact #55:

The human body requires iron to perform a number of important functions. Iron helps carry oxygen to parts of your body in the form of hemoglobin.

The human body requires iron to

perform a number of important

functions. Iron helps carry oxygen

to parts of your body in the form of

hemoglobin.

Science Fact #56:

Red blood cells are created inside the bone marrow.

Red blood cells are created inside the

bone marrow.

Science Fact #57:
Antibiotics can be useful in fighting off bacteria but they are ineffective against viruses.

Antibiotics can be useful in fighting
off bacteria but they are ineffective
against viruses.

Science Fact #58:

Around 2% of adults and 8% of children suffer from some type of food allergy. This type of reaction happens when the immune system makes a mistake and thinks a certain food protein is dangerous and attacks it.

Around 2% of adults and 8% of children suffer from some type of food allergy. This type of reaction happens when the immune system makes a mistake and thinks a certain food protein is dangerous and attacks it.

Science Fact #59:

It's believed that humans began to use fire for cooking food in a controlled way around 1 million years ago.

It's believed that humans began to

use fire for cooking food in a

controlled way around 1 million

years ago.

Science Fact #60:
A candle flame burns at around 1000 degrees Celsius.

A candle flame burns at around
1000 degrees Celsius.

The word 'nuclear' is related to the nucleus of an atom.

The word 'nuclear' is related to the

nucleus of an atom.

Science Fact #62:
The nucleus is found at the central core of an atom and is
positively charged.

The nucleus is found at the central
core of an atom and is positively
charged.

Science Fact #63 :

The largest producers of nuclear power are the USA, France and Japan.

The largest producers of nuclear power are the USA, France and Japan.

Science Fact #64:
The Titanic was 269 meters (882 feet) long.

The Titanic was 269 meters (882 feet)

long.

Science Fact #65:
The first coins were made approximately 2500 years ago.

The first coins were made

approximately 2500 years ago.

Science Fact #66:
Paper money was first used over 1000 years ago in China.

Paper money was first used over 1000
years ago in China.

Science Fact #67:
Lightning bolts can reach almost 30,000°C (54,000 °F) in temperature while traveling at around 210,000 kph (130,000 mph).

Lightning bolts can reach almost 30,000°C (54,000 °F) in temperature while traveling at around 210,000 kph (130,000 mph).

Science Fact #68:
Kinetic energy refers to the energy an object possesses because of its movement.

Kinetic energy refers to the energy an object possesses because of its movement.

The law of conservation of energy states that energy can only be transformed – it cannot be created or destroyed.

The law of conservation of energy
states that energy can only be
transformed – it cannot be created
or destroyed.

Science Fact #70:
Nuclear power produces around 13%-14% of the world's electricity.

Nuclear power produces around
13%-14% of the world's electricity.

Science Fact #71:
Tungsten has the second-highest melting point of all elements,
after carbon.

Tungsten has the second-highest

melting point of all elements, after

carbon.

Science Fact #72:

Bronze is a metal alloy created from copper and tin.

Bronze is a metal alloy created

from copper and tin.

Science Fact #73:
The brain uses over a quarter of the oxygen used by the entire human body.

The brain uses over a quarter of the

oxygen used by the entire human

body.

Science Fact #74:

In addition to having unique fingerprints, humans also have unique tongue prints.

In addition to having unique

fingerprints, humans also have

unique tongue prints.

Science Fact #75:

Recycling plastic can be more difficult than other materials.
Plastics are not typically recycled into the same type of plastic.

Recycling plastic can be more difficult
than other materials. Plastics are not
typically recycled into the same type
of plastic.

Science Fact #76:
Recycling old aluminum uses only 5% of the energy needed to make new aluminum.

Recycling old aluminum uses only
5% of the energy needed to make new
aluminum.

Science Fact #77:
Glass is often separated into colors because it retains its color after recycling.

Glass is often separated into colors
because it retains its color after
recycling.

Science Fact #78:

For every ton of recycled glass, 315 kilograms of carbon dioxide
that would have been released during the creation of new glass
is saved.

For every ton of recycled glass, 315
kilograms of carbon dioxide that
would have been released during the
creation of new glass is saved.

Science Fact #79:
Hydrogen is the most common element found in the universe.

Hydrogen is the most common
element found in the universe.

Science Fact #80:

Approximately 1% of the sun's mass is made up of oxygen.

Approximately 1% of the sun's mass

is made up of oxygen.

Science Fact #81:

Above 4 °C, water expands when heated and contracts when cooled. However, between 4 °C and 0 °C it does the opposite, contracting when heated and expanding when cooled.

Above 4 °C, water expands when

heated and contracts when cooled.

However, between 4 °C and 0 °C it

does the opposite, contracting when

heated and expanding when cooled.

Science Fact #82:

The heaviest hailstone ever recorded weighed around 1.0 kg (2.25 lb.) and landed in the Gopalganj District, Bangladesh on April 14, 1986.

The heaviest hailstone ever recorded weighed around 1.0 kg (2.25 lb.) and landed in the Gopalganj District, Bangladesh on April 14, 1986.

Science Fact #83:

Tornadoes are not always visible. However, high wind speeds and rapid rotation form a visible funnel of condensed water.

Tornadoes are not always visible.

However, high wind speeds and rapid

rotation form a visible funnel of

condensed water.

Science Fact #84:

The Fujita Scale is a common way of measuring the strength of tornadoes. It ranges from F0 (tornadoes that cause minimal damage) to F5 (tornadoes that cause massive damage).

The Fujita Scale is a common way of
measuring the strength of tornadoes.
It ranges from F0 (tornadoes that
cause minimal damage) to F5
(tornadoes that cause massive
damage).

Science Fact #85:
Extreme tornadoes can reach wind speeds of over 300 miles per hour (483 kilometres per hour).

Extreme tornadoes can reach wind speeds of over 300 miles per hour (483 kilometres per hour).

Science Fact #86:
Extreme tornadoes can sometimes travel a distance of over 100 miles (161 kilometres).

Extreme tornadoes can sometimes travel a distance of over 100 miles (161 kilometres).

Science Fact #87:
The adult human skeleton is made up of 206 bones.

The adult human skeleton is made up of 206 bones.

Science Fact #88:
The thigh bone, called the femur, is the longest bone in the
human body.

The thigh bone, called the femur, is
the longest bone in the human body.

Science Fact #89:

The hand, fingers and wrist contain a total of 54 bones. It is the area of the human body with the most bones.

The hand, fingers and wrist contain a total of 54 bones. It is the area of the human body with the most bones.

Science Fact #90:

The female skeleton is generally slightly smaller than that of a male, and the pelvis bones differ in shape, size and angle to assist with childbirth.

The female skeleton is generally
slightly smaller than that of a male,
and the pelvis bones differ in shape,
size and angle to assist with
childbirth.

Science Fact #91 :

The majority of human bones have a dense, strong outer layer, along with a spongy part full of air for lightness. The middle section contains a soft, flexible tissue substance called bone marrow.

The majority of human bones have

a dense, strong outer layer, along

with a spongy part full of air for

lightness. The middle section contains

a soft, flexible tissue substance called

bone marrow.

Science Fact #92 :

Bone marrow makes up 4% of human body mass. The bone marrow is also responsible for producing lymphocytes, key components of the lymphatic system that support the body's immune system.

Bone marrow makes up 4% of
human body mass. The bone marrow
is also responsible for producing
lymphocytes, key components of the
lymphatic system that support the
body's immune system.

Made in the USA
Coppell, TX
19 September 2022

83366776R00057